JOETRY IN MOTION

Joseph Campling

Cover photograph
Jofuss Camelyne

Illustrations
Photographs by Jofuss Camelyne
Copyright © 2022 Joseph Campling
All rights reserved.
No parts of this publication may be reproduced, stored in a retrieval system, or transmitted in any form or by any means, electronic, mechanical, photocopying, recording, or otherwise, without the prior written permission of the copyright owner.
This book is sold subject to the condition that it shall not, by way of trade or otherwise, be lent, resold, hired out, or otherwise circulated without the publisher's prior consent in any form of binding or cover other than that in which it is published and without a similar condition including this condition being imposed on the subsequent purchaser. Under no circumstances may any part of this book be photocopied for resale.

ISBN-13:
9798541832914

DEDICATION

Poetry in Motion
Johnny Tillotson 1961

INTRODUCTION

Why the title of the book?

Well, mid pandemic I celebrated a birthday, and one notification was a portmanteau of my name with the song title.

I vaguely knew the chorus but have looked into the 'song' itself
The song is about a stream of women which the writer saw walking in front of him every afternoon and was his 'tribute' to their differences.

The song also references another song "Love Potion No 9" which I suppose links tangentially by my writing based on listening to music and the use of influences from all around me to stimulate my mind.

I celebrate that I have survived to continue writing, and I celebrate that I am able not just to write these words, but to share in public again.

Over the past few months, I have managed to link up in person with my fellow writers / wordsmiths / performers, some of whom I knew before lockdown and wonderfully with some new whom I met for the first time via Zoom or MS Teams.

My reflections are about my feelings around poetry in my life. Poetry for me is not a stagnant process, it is always evolving and bringing the old and the new together into a new creation.
I find words are very powerful but also so seductive and they draw me into them. I find my own conscious and unconscious meanings in them and that that keeps me mentally healthy.

Sometimes there are words I have shared and sometimes I reflect the hidden thoughts that writing them down helps to rationalise and make sense of them.
Poetry helps me share a part of me that I didn't know existed. I

always thought of myself as a scientific person but in reality, it was the artful side cementing that together.

I keep moving forward in this art, so I am really "Joetry in Motion"

ACKNOWLEDGEMENTS

As when writing my previous books, I have continued to be influenced by what I see, hear or feel around me. These lines are a shout out to them.

As always, the guys who let me perform my words. The various Open Mics and Spoken Word events over past two years in and out of lockdown

I need to acknowledge Carmel who was one of the first to allow me to perform and also bought my books.
I acknowledge that support and the sadness of her passing.

I acknowledge the support of the Innerverse and our writing group which has just started up to allow us to learn and to share our written work.

I close my acknowledgements with love to my family as they still put up with me spouting words at them, or at least not complaining to my face!!

FIND ME

Twitter @CamplingJoe

Instagram campling.joe

https://joecamplingpoetry.com

FRIDAY

It is the end of the week

Time to start the process of relaxing

It is Friday

TGIF

Maybe I will be able to sleep in tomorrow

As it is Saturday

But we are not there yet as the parent says to the child on one of those long car journeys

We still have hours to go

So, what is Friday about?

Is it to do with all that fish that was fried when I was young?

This was accompanied by agricultural chips.

Not those little matches that are all vogue at takeaways

But no

It is to do with the Vikings of the past.

They brought their Norse ways

When they invaded the lands

Or was it the other pirates with an 'angle'

Those were also known as the Saxons.

They threw out the Brits

And declared new days

They commemorate the fair Frigga or Freya

Instead of the Roman Venus

Still being European

And expressing the love of the good women.

From both traditions

So, to recap

Friday is about decent food, relaxation and celebrating love

TOILET

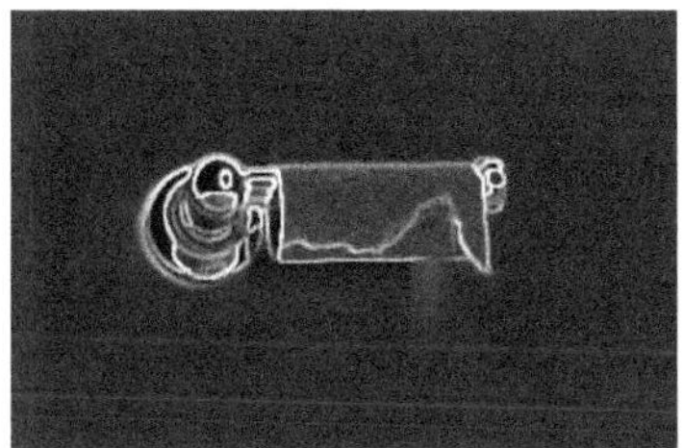

Time on the toilet

I sit and wait for the ultimate ridding of waste

It gives me time to reflect

Just me time

The four walls

My brain

My thoughts

Just waiting

A load off my mind

As I put the world to rights

And I just wander off for a while

Into a relaxation mode

Away from the madness behind the door

I do not even need to eliminate

Just to articulate to myself

That I have this time

That precious commodity

That is mine

But was forgotten

As I hid it in mediocrity

Of someone else's making

Except they did not know

I just projected my failure onto them

Time to flush so I can meet the world again

STORM

The crash of thunder

An enormous kettle drum being beaten by the gods above

The heavenly furniture is being moved about

As the air crackles into lightning

One of the gods is flickering with the electrics

Banging to scare off the evil spirits

The bright flash lights the way

Another one forms a fork above

Something turned on a shower from above

Its torrents pour as it initially soaks

And then destroys the sodden tent

Hardy scouts have taken their chance

And have been caught out

They huddle clothes useless against the cold liquid

Which will not stop pouring down

They start to make plans to run away

But initially they are too hesitant

Suddenly despite being sodden they bravely dash from the fallen cover

The rusty minibus ahead will be a temporary shelter

So that they can await the cessation of the downpour

As suddenly as it started all is silent

A shaft of sun through the still falling rain

A curve of colour above tempting you to search for the pot of gold

It is all over till next time

MUTANT

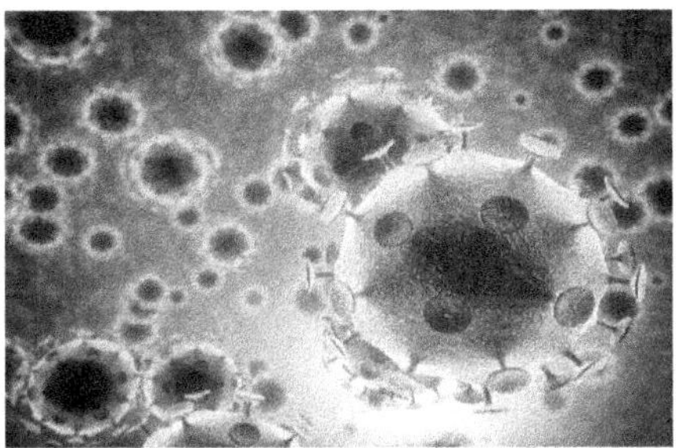

From the outset it seemed normal

Life as we knew it

But hidden away was a change

Something that no one had thought could exist

It was unexplained

It clung onto life and grew

Instead of dying away

The thing we did not want

Made its way through the world

Attaching itself to the disadvantaged

And those who had everything

Not differentiating good or bad

Just being

The scientists gave it a name

It drove fear into the masses

The politicians downplayed its significance

Saying that they were in charge

That it was no risk

Then they listened to the science

And changed the plans

Told the population to stay at home

Not panic

Making the rules

Keep safe

Not always abiding by them

Allowing the instinct for the mighty

Punishing the weak

Ridiculing the strong

Sharing the misinformation

Along with the truth

Still, nobody knows the answer

As the beast may bite back

It may gather pace again

Rear up its ugly head

As it is not subdued yet

Just being pacified

Or just changing its skin

So, it may stealthily reappear

And not be revealed

Until it attacks again

CRIMINAL MINDS

I am going to fool you

I have a keen mind and am intellectually more superior

My crime will go undetected as I am so clever.

You will not know it was me or have any connection to anything

You will discover too late what I have done

That is if you do so

I will not make the mistake of being too overconfident for my own good

That is when my vulnerabilities will become clear.

Who knows?

I will get away with it

I still have not let you know what IT is

That is my secret.

I sneak around behind people's backs

I enact my con

And you do not know

I am a genius

Oh dear boasting too much

I had better be quiet

As evil deeds get found out.

Except, I do not want to be around when you find out.

Stop talking

The blue light approaches

ADULT

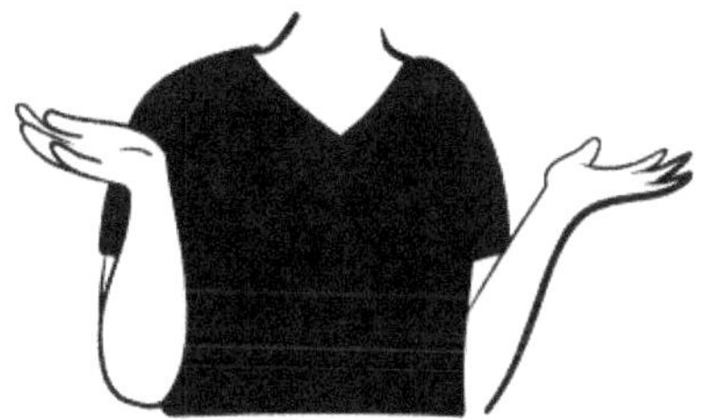

One day l awoke

I realized that it came upon me

By stealth it crept into my head

The sudden change from childhood

I am an adult

I do not know how it happened

Nothing else changed

It was just another day

Like all the others

Except I now became responsible

Was I irresponsible before?

Because no one told me I was

I was growing up nicely

Reaching maturity at my own pace

However, the state of adulthood was thrust upon me

I was eighteen

I could make decisions

I could drink alcohol

Buy a porn mag

These were not things that I wanted to do daily

But they were now available to me

This now longer child was free to indulge in vices

That had been restricted to me

For either health or morality

And I was now licensed to be as drunk as I wanted

Because I was now responsible

With my day older liver and my increased sexual experience

Of time

Executed by legal purposes

But not taking account of my innocence

Of the harsh world

I had been sheltered from

So, I get up

Relish the singing of Happy Birthday

And realize

I have a bit longer to choose

Which way my life goes

As I do not need to rush

To either ruin my life

Or have influence

SPECSAVERS

DC sneaks out of the door, looking feverishly for paparazzi in case he is discovered not to be in his sickbed directing things.

"Just get into the car to celebrate your birthday. That's it strap yourselves in so we can make a day of it."

Mrs DC checks "are you feeling ok to drive?"

"We'll soon see when I get behind the wheel "the erstwhile spin-doctor responds.

Hopefully, the boy's well.

Checking the odometer to confirm distance travelled is 25 miles.

Welcome to Castle Barnard aka Specsavers.

Flash forward, so tell them this truth Boris, I can see clearly now

LIVERPOOL

It all began in Germany where a small revolution occurred when he shared his message.

It then moved around the country where the dogma began to make headway.

There was initial success, but it faltered at the last hurdle against the Bavarians

When he was free, another city saw his potential and the leader was able to enact his plan

European domination.

For the leader, the long-term desire England was always just out of reach

2020 changed all that

Word to the wise Stan Boardman they did not bomb your chip shop

They battered the others.

King Klopp of the Kop

COVID HAIR

Covid hair grows everywhere

Strange styles for the world to wear

Some of us let it grow free

Others behave like life's severe

Styling faces with a shave

Or removing it so brave

Waiting for the barber to open

But sadly, you need to join the list that goes on

A virtual trim is what I need

Because I am not consumed with greed

For the usual short back and sides of old

Paid with the old legal tender of paper and faux gold

FRUIT

It is mid-summer.

The trees are starting to be fruitful.

What can be seen are the buds of apples as they continue to grow

The blossoms have all faded away- well mostly

A few blooms are clear as the student has waited for this day- the dawning of the results

A passage in life which has been part of a longer life goal

To attend a place of higher learning

A new act of activity

This will be an opportunity to change their horizon.

They are aware that this has been a strange year.

Their preparation for the dreaded exams was cancelled so instead their treasured crop will be harvested vicariously

They have lost their personal control as the farmer of their destiny, but they trust what they have been told, they have been made promises

The seeds that they had planted in their halls of study should have bloomed naturally for all to see.

However just as it was supposed to have come to fruition- to mature

The flowers were deadheaded

Some were not yet fully formed

But hopefully there was still enough fruit remaining on the tree

For those gourmets to taste

To classify the vintage

To share the essence and to give hope

The experts had shown them the way but sadly the growers were unable to evaluate their own resilience

As this was a strange season for the tending of their growing produce

With odd weather- gusts of danger blowing around their communities

But suddenly the rules had changed

A new way of grading the apples

And some were saying that they were pears

All dependent on changing the ABC's.

Renaming the variety

Pushed through an algorithm of some faceless making

This prejudiced some of the newer orchards.

And the higher seats of learning became graded superior as in a supermarket war

And some of the buyers started to reject the produce

For no rhyme nor reason

As if it had been marked as not fit for purpose although it was initially labelled as excellent

It might as well have had a big sticker saying damaged

As it was thrown into the cheap baskets of life

For someone to hopefully grab the remnants

But like in the Garden of Eden

Beware of knowledge from serpents

Who make false promises

Suddenly wisdom was alighting up those apples and pears

The quality of the produce had been mislabelled after all

A higher power realised that something was up

Political expediency snaked a stream of light to the growers and the harvesters

Opened the eyes of learning to the new market purchasers.

That the pears were also fruit

That they could be used like apples

And their sweetness remained valid.

And who knows

Next year there will be a new crop of apples

That will be juicy just like the pears

LOST IN TRANSLATION

There we were in the darkness after the Christmas party.

I remember how happy I was when I think back about that time of year.

I think especially about the darkness of the afternoons

I do not even know what it is about the winter, but everything has changed since then.

This remarkable woman separated the light and darkness from the varying scattered parts of my life.

I was not aware when it came upon me suddenly

I felt a completely different extreme strange feeling.

But as soon as it came, it was gone again in an instant

I felt surrounded by its magic

The feelings sank into me like I was drowning in its essence.

I was immersed

I felt like she was treating me with something secret that was so indescribable.

I became dizzy and emotional

Questioning where are you tonight?

I felt sad when she left my life so quickly, or I was wrong and, in fact, she left me later

BEAR/BARE

Exit stage left pursued by a bear

What did the bear think about it?

Why was he chasing?

Was he wanting to bare his soul about being locked up prior to the performance

Not able to make his views known

Who listens to a bear anyway?

Most just grab it in their arms and hold tight.

Giving the proverbial bear hug.

Squeezing the life out of you

Did he kill Antigonus on purpose or was it an unplanned exit

These and other questions are still unfulfilled through the ages

Who or what was the bear and what did he stand for?

A question

Was he at that stage in life where he was left?

Left behind from what he believed in

Or was he right

No, he definitely left

Left in the wings

Left wing which we know can be right

In the correct circumstances

As it ran from the stage bringing an end to something sacred

Or am I confusing myself

And making excuses for something of which I know nothing

Except I do -I do not go for this faux nationalism

By that 'cuddly toy' pm we have

Who everyone thought had exited the stage.

Instead, he caused us to exit instead

Backbiting each other divide and rule

For their political drool

Baiting our neighbours

In the pit of despair that is politics

Treading on the bones of what went before us

As though it did not matter.

Creating a different Shakespearean drama

Our own winter's tale

BANANAS

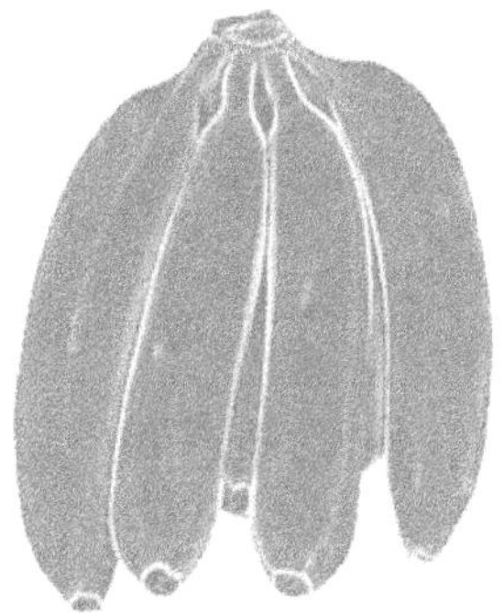

Thinking about the yellow fruit

It has such uses in the vernacular

Like treading on its carapace is a mistake

And making like the dessert and getting the hell out of here

But it makes its own mythology

Like the EU rules about its angle of bend

And it needing to be of a certain length

Who knew that Fyffes would want a monopoly?

On the crates and the boats that brought them here.

The joy on the post war children's face

That a fruit could be so bright

And yet the banana boat fed into the national conscious

As a term of abuse of being seen as not from round here.

We hope that the sweetness will overcome

As the nutrition oozes into the mortal being

And memories of the joy

And the children

Bring a smile to the face

As mashed up with sugar made the tea party complete

Between two slices of the daily loaf

Culinary fusion in its infancy

CARNIVOROUS SURFING

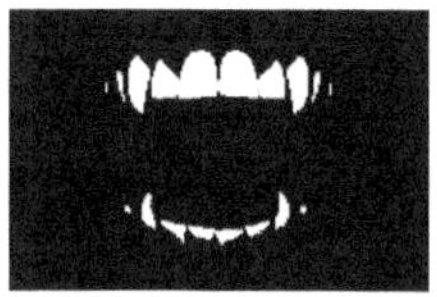

We spend all our lives waiting for excitement to happen

We do not know which knife we should sharpen

We think of living as a given

Believing that we will eventually go to our heaven

Instead, we are beholden to the birds of prey

Wanting to find us everyday

We hide ourselves from them as they seek to make their meal complete

Those virtual eagles circling overhead looking for the rotting meat

They do not know what they may find

They also do not want to be left behind

They search intently with their beady eyes

Hoping that they have the element of surprise

This constant surveillance not self-imposed

As we comment continuously about our journey along life's road

And post tomes upon the social media

We are self-appointed experts on the digital encyclopaedia

Spending time arguing the toss with our friends

And then backtracking trying to make amends

With thumbs up and likes upon the page

Getting stuck in generating rage

The carrion crows just eat the scraps

As the ordinary world collapsed

People are too scared to express their thoughts

As it is assumed that they are up to all sorts

And crime itself has not diminished

But humanity will soon be finished

The apocalypse it is now

As the moon jumps over the cow

But we will deny the wilderness beyond us

And climb onto the sacred minibus

CHRISTMAS LOCKDOWN

We have been locked up for Christmas

Do I spend my time trying to find out who I will hold responsible for letting us out of this 2020 nightmare?

I do not remember committing any of the crimes for which humanity is being punished

Except potentially was it my pride- the deadliest sin or was it just falling for consumerism?

The usual exercise of pushing ourselves around the shops splashing the cash or increasing the credit card debt

Instead, I look around as everyone else is moving about aimlessly on the streets

No direction left

Running likes hamsters on their wheel fomenting plans of escape

But not really getting anywhere

Do I start making plans as the diverse options for release are explored?

Do I wait for changes in the environmental tiers?

As the salty tears just run like torrential rain down my cheeks in increasing sadness

Do I just complain that I cannot see the kids who I encourage to be independent?

They have their own lives now

Am I trying to encourage them to become dependent again?

Is it my selfishness or self-interest I look to feed?

Do I instead fill myself up with sweets and other carbohydrates that the yuletide celebrations demand?

Does this make me feel good as I wait for the deliciousness of the pheromones in dark chocolate to ooze their wash over me?

Do I give myself red meat constipation so I can complain of having had a 'real Christmas log' this year?

Maybe I should just get blind drunk and let everyone know what I think of them.

Ventilate cathartically or just be angry.

Like I would do that!!

I will just hold my tongue as I do not see the value in imbibing alcohol that often

Maybe I'll just have to make a New Year resolution to atone for this sin of false witness against my fellow struggler

And just remember that it is Christmas time

Bathe in the glory of the spiritual experience

Realise that life is not as bad as my negativity makes out because I am still breathing

I have many sets of people who are happy to call themselves my family and friends

We have made a blood pact

We will eventually be free again

We all understand the need for good behaviour

And we will regain our parole on the other side.

ACROSTIC

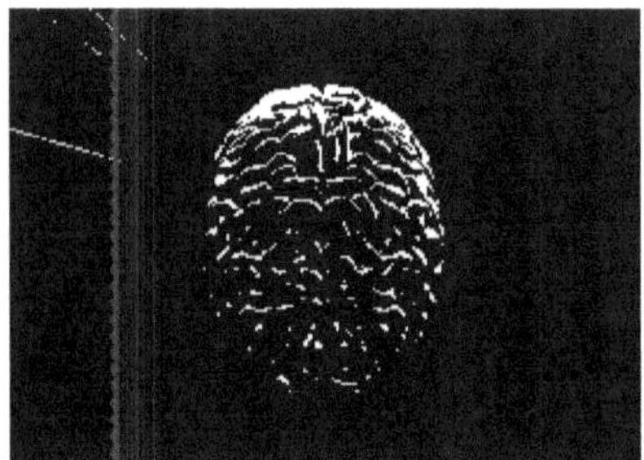

Behold! - I have your destiny in my mighty hands

Ruler from the vile kingdom below beware

It is from divine and earthly forces that I cast my powerful spell on you

Shake with fear at my magnificence

Hide yourself from my anger as my wrath is unforgiving

No one who takes a stand is exempt from my vengeance

Alone you make your defences against me

Seemingly aggrieved you stand erect against me

Honour me- you mockingly make your demands

As you feel that you are omnipotent enough defy me

Ha-ha I roar with laughter- I will crush you, I am more powerful than you believe

VERBAL LASHING

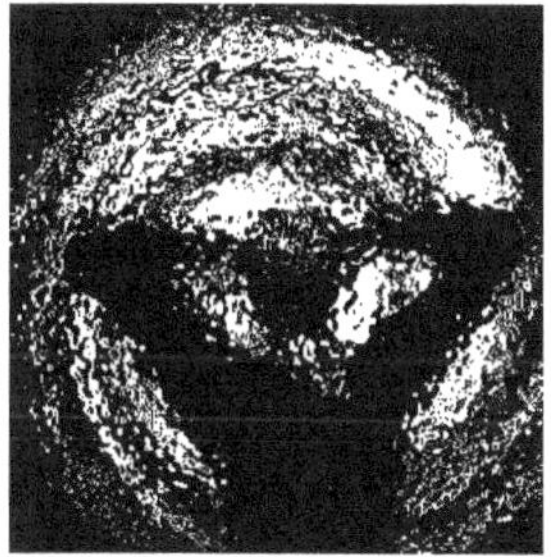

We see ourselves as the face of God

Created in his image

But we feel that we too have been forsaken.

Causing us to have cognitive dissonance

Which cannot reconcile by just sleeping it off.

Remember that we are mere mortals

We crash, iconoclasts railing against the perceived norms

We must remember that one day we will die

In the service of ourselves or the others

We live to the ideals pressed upon us or continue this mental fight

The dichotomy of thoughts making us uneasy within our mortal flesh

We must challenge -shout out the message of power

But who told us to do so -where does it come from?

The invisible voices of love restrain us with bonds of life

As we make our way along the journey to the terminus

We remember to listen to the instructions and try to understand what we must do

They seem that they are spoken in a foreign tongue

An unrecognisable language

But they pierce like the barbs of a lance

They inject their meaning deeply

Like a vaccine of deliverance

Remember that we are mortal continues to race through our confused mind

Exciting pathways of electricity which we cannot control

Flagellation of the self by magic words

WANDERING MIND

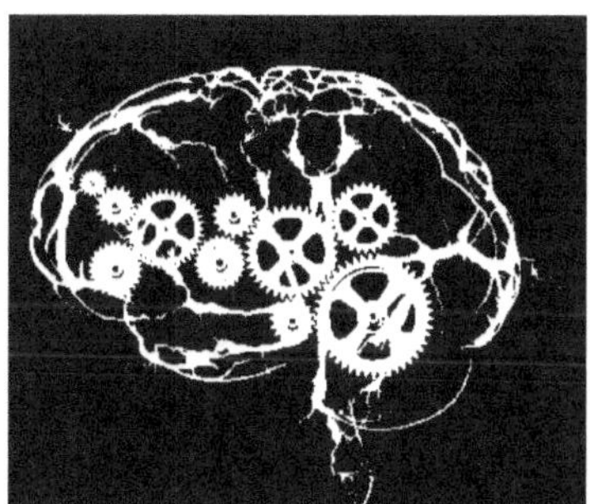

Jauntily I let those thoughts wander through my unconscious mind

Opening up my fragility to others

Slipping away from the reality of consciousness into a stupor of chemical haze

Exaggerating the validity of those doubts which you are expressing to me

Punishing yourself for the changes that I refuse to make at your behest

Hallelujah, you want to sing at my redemption

Clambering onto the passing celestial chariot that swings on by as you save me

Amazed that you will be able to bathe in the divinity of your rescuing behaviour

Mortality will no longer have to sting you like a vexatious wasp as a reminder

Painful memories of me being a distant river as it ebbs away into the oblivion of a new dawn

Life is not over but it will have everyone's support to begins its cycle again

Instantly prayers resound melodically from the assembled throng for the succour of your soul

Narcissism from my actions no longer tearing at your being

Gladness soaking into the material of your living and not your spiritual death

SYMPTOM CONTROL

Cough cough she said

Open up your mouth

Reach right in with the swab

Our task is to identify whether something is wrong

Naturally, we know all too well given the symptoms

Actively pursuing our diagnosis with vigour

Violence by the virus against the body imperfect

Inhaled without a care against your will unknowingly

Rasping breaths, the outcome

Upsetting the normality of family life

Stay away

LONG SERVICE

Please carry on working

At this moment we need your experience

Time spent with you reflects what we need

Reproach us not for these words

Intertwined with my respect

Clad in years of love

Independence still paramount

At the behest of your professionalism

Jousting with others for your attention

On all days of the week, month year

Harvesting the spoils of your riches over the decades

Noting what is real and unreal

WELTSCHMERZ

Who am I?

Where am I?

I have crawled into this alternative world of pain

There is a familiarity in the air, but all is not the same

I vaguely recognise the people in front of me, but they are haunted by the spectre of the present

They see a blank future inhabited by ghosts of earlier acquaintances well known

I see the landmarks and visions which should guide me from A to B

Except I do not know which direction I am to go

All seems lost

B seems to have turned to C and A is closed

Life has changed as we know it and we are told that we aspire to the new normality

I see that there are spurts of growth, but as green shoots appear they are stunted or removed quickly

We have hit the end of the pier show

The performers are singing their songs

But instead of joy and fun they spout destruction of their former normal

All that we knew previously

A political joke and spin doctors

Telling everyone it is ok but to hang on

They wear their smart suits

Smile politely at the questions

But the reality is different

The mental skin is ripped away like a cheap veneer

Exposing that there is pain beneath

The rawness of a perceived vitality

Hoping that a scab will form to allow healing

Instead, the toxic atmosphere tugs away at it

Picking at the temporary repair

The damage stays uppermost for the world to see

We hope for better things

The scar will form and that will be the evidence that we have survived

Finding our direction again from the ruins left behind

A new world will appear from the ashes

Like an ethereal reality

The survivors will pick up the pieces

And government ministers will explain how they did it

Like a new chapter from 1984

RED SKY

Red sky at night

Picking the fight

Red sky in the morning

Blood is pouring

Red sky at night

Bonfire is alight

Red sky in the morning

Political issues boring

Red sky in the day

Continue with bigotry

Red sky in the evening

History repeating

Red sky in the afternoon

Repeated cross community doom

Red sky everywhere

Incendiary bombs and flares

Red sky in your brain

Not learning from your pain

Red sky is full of smoke

Continued violence and death are no joke

Red blood on the ground

Looks like we are on the unforgiving merry go round

Red lines in the sand

Forgive and move on

The End

PANDEMIC BLUES

Woke up one day in March

Switched on the news

Made me feel so sad

Pandemic blues

Pubs and shops all shut

Nothing to do

Lost in transit

Pandemic blues

Increasing the lockdown

People cannot go to work

Staying at home overcrowding

Pandemic jerks

Random PCR tests

Needing to be safe

Keeping on top of the situation

Pandemic time starts to chafe

Infection rates are lower

Things start to reopen again

Eating out to save the world

Pandemic gain down the drain

Time for education

Kids all go to school

Lockdown down back in the North

Pandemic is so cruel

Promised we will meet for Christmas

Counting down the days

Death rates increase again

Pandemic holiday pain

Here comes the injection

Time to get immune

Weird feelings for a day

Pandemic over by June

Do not be complacent

We will be together soon

Keep swallowing the hard medicine

Pandemic on the wain

BIRTHDAY

Today is my birthday

Do I look grey

Waiting for the cards and presents hurray

Will it be like every other day

Sit on my backside and pray

For the coming retirement day

Is much closer my thoughts betray

Songs from the jukebox telling me to walk this way

When all I want to do is go to bed and lay

And look at my app for my monthly pay

And watch the money depart with no delay

I see my pessimism gets in the way

Of all the joy I should have today

I have reached a milestone, so they say

And I will cut my cake on this special day

HI, I'M YOUR NURSE IN SO MANY WORDS

(As I am your nurse)

Hi, I am a nurse

Are you inspired to think what that means to you?

Do you think about the care you want?

Or the care you may have had in the past

Is it about how hard it has been for the last year?

How I have shared this struggle with you

How the world you knew has changed around you and me

Hi, I'm still here as your nurse

We are keeping it normal together

Well as normal as it can be as "whoever defined normal in the first place?"

I am happily sharing the burden of keeping you safe.

I try to communicate this to you under my mask

Show you that I still can care

Trying my best to at least make my eyes smile!

I may have been around a long time

But our reality is I still learn from you

So, by saying "Hi I'm your nurse"

I aim to share your health experiences with you

Good and bad

I am not here to judge but forgive my slips as I am a human too!

I aim to go with you when you make your journey

Pressing my feet into your footsteps as you guide along the way

Sharing what we come across together

And I am your nurse, and you know my name

Not a faceless masked entity around you

Hi, I'm still your nurse

Are you still thinking?

You can see me

You can talk to me

As I have dedicated my life to looking out for you

Because that is what it means to be a nurse

It is important for you to know

I may have studied to an important level

Have letters after my name

Gained knowledge about the technical aspects of care

I am so proud of this

But what matters comes from within me

And it is what I have to share with you

The important part of me

That makes us a whole

And I will make the effort to help you to understand this

As I make the effort to understand you

Keeping this candle lit for future generations

And reflecting on those who have been before me

Who have been a positive influence for me

As I loudly trumpet, I am your nurse

And I will always be your nurse

Jestem twoją pielęgniarką

Maadaama aan ahay kalkaaliyahaaga caafimaad

Wie bin ich Ihre Krankenschwester.

Comme je suis votre infirmière

ਹੋਣ ਦੇ ਨਾਤੇ, ਮੈਨੂੰ ਆਪਣੇ ਨਰਸ ਹੈ.

DELAYED START

We had our hopes for 2020

The football will go so well for the Euros

Liverpool will wipe the floor with the other Premier League Teams

We have done our Olympic qualifiers and will see you soon in Tokyo

I wonder who will win Wimbledon?

They will climb Murray Mount (renamed from Henman Hill and Rusedski Ridge) and eat overpriced strawberries and drink champagne

Will there be controversy at Glastonbury when bands will be reported for drug taking

Or it will be all washed out and everyone will be singing in the rain.

Except that did not happen.

On a wave of cannot do this for now

Euro 2020 cancelled till next year

Liverpool still won the League but did not break the records

Olympics cancelled till next year- Sayonara

No Wimbledon

No Glastonbury

Even no Eurovision- except the Will Ferrell fantasy film

Like the First World War, it was all supposed be over for Christmas

Except it all started again

Christmas was cancelled (except virtually)

We ate our minimalised turkey dinner with less pudding

We sang Auld Lang Syne and Zoomed or Skyped as these worlds became our normality

We calculated if we could meet up and who was allowed and swore or praised the Government response to what we wanted

But it still went on

We were mitigated by our COVID jab which would equal freedom.

So as things get back to normal or we could vicariously watch on TV

The world has had its Eurovision

UK null point

Happy Junemas, pull the crackers

Murray is out of Wimbledon

The football went Man City, Chelsea, and Leicester's way

But 3 Lions seems to mean a little more.

Or is it Sweet Caroline

The nation watching the sport

Even if it is the promised bank holiday for a win.

Is this the start of a return to normality

A reflection of the new normal!!

Or are we on the Magic Roundabout again

Time for bed everyone!

It is time for the adults to watch the news.

EMERGING BIRTHDAY

Another year over within this hell

A new one with joyous stories to tell

Thoughts and brilliant plans are soon in place

The author photo now has a smile on his face

But firstly, imagining tastes of various brews

I wish a fellow wordsmith "happy birthday to you"

MUSIC

Music feeds your soul

Who knows when you will get a meal like that?

It is not McDonalds but Cordon Bleu

Unless a takeaway is what you need

The words like rare steak

Easily cut and beautiful to the palate

Or a lovely veggie alternative

As we all cannot be carnivores

That is the wonder of music

You can choose from the menu to find something to your taste

Or you can experiment and take a risk

Some are born with knowing the recipes and ingredients

Some have the skills

Some work hard to make the effort as an amateur

Or some are Master chefs or is that 'Master clefs'

The noises are sweet and melodious

Or just loud and banging

The beat goes on or gets staccato and stops

But it sows its seeds its seeds in your soul

And it grows and grows

The flora produced is wonderous

And the musical horticulturist harvests the blooms

And shares the gifts to the room

LIFE THROUGH THE BOTTOM OF A GLASS

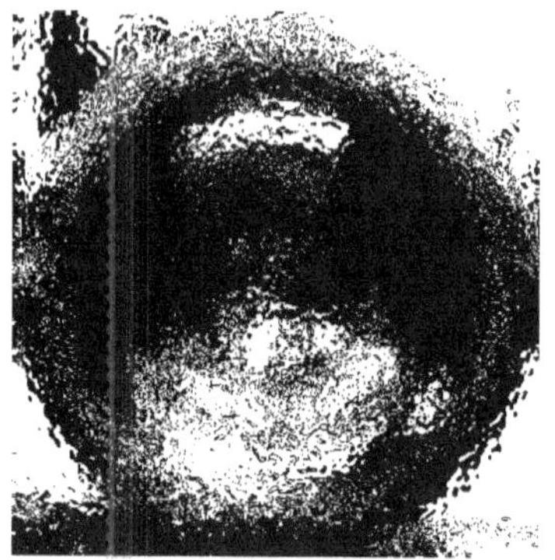

I examine my life through the bottom of a glass

It is amber coloured and bubble framed

The world bordered by its gorgeous glow

It feels so good to be looking ahead of me at the people in front

The occasional froth cloud floating by

Creating hairpieces to change their appearances momentarily

The buzz of people's conversations

And the laughter rings pleasantly around my head

I take a second chance to examine life around me

The same amber outline

This however is more muted, and I am feeling quieter

I muse over the changes

My emotions are stilted- more controlled

I feel I can incise life's problems like a surgeon

I am the answer to your prayers

I take a third and fourth chemically induced view around me

The clouds over people's heads are less prominent

The wonderful conversation is like tinnitus to my ears

So annoying and will not go away

What they are saying is so wrong -I still have the taste for auditing life

I imbibe my fifth fuel injection

The bottom of the glass no longer soft clouds

But hard liquor- thick and viscous

I convince myself that I need a more powerful argument

And rocket fuel will be the answer

I hear my 'gift of the gab' in my auditory processes

As I vocalise my truth

Instead, I suddenly feel a stinging pain in my face

The bottom of someone else's glass

Who felt I needed to heed his world view

The outcome was the optical illusion of a blood red sea

Which changed my experience of life forever

GROWING UP

Reflected in the pool of life

A splash produces ripples upon the earth

From the tiny seed to shoot you were nurtured as you grew up

You were now a towering staff of power and knowledge

Which was needed to leave and make your way in the world

You collect your belongings from around you to ensure that you have a stability wherever you land

To protect you from the pests who try to steal your goodness

So, you can continue to flourish and produce blooms

You can share your elegance

Your ethereal beauty is loved by all

Happiness is your fruit which you happily embed in others

It makes them shines with glory

You now investigate the new pool in front of you to see your changed reflection

The pain feeds your growth as you expand your metaphorical shoots further into another place

The potential growth is fed by the confidence of others

The plans are in place to ensure that stems are stable

And further growth is encouraged unabated

Your smile is as beautiful as a sunflower, and it radiates its joyfulness from you

As you plan your next journey

QUEUEING

John looked at the throng of people in front of him and he sighed aloud.

I have to fill myself up at the pump to keep myself going.

Slowly the snake in front moved along a couple of feet and he braced himself as he got closer to the people in front.

Suddenly there was a swerve from the left. Another decided that their need was greater.

Oi, you stupid bleep as his words were drowned out by others. Wait your turn and join the queue like everyone else.

I want my lager and lime and I want it now

TIMOR LESTE

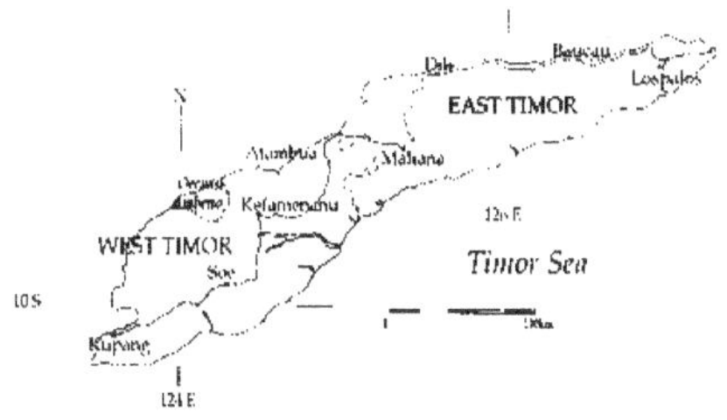

An excited young man from Timor Leste

Discovered he had food stains on his vest

So, he removed all the offensive clothes

And was getting ready to dispose

But realised it was only a birthmark on his chest

The young man from Timor Leste

Decided that he would like to go West

So, wetting his finger in his mouth

He figured out what was South

And then spoiled his science as he just guessed

THE FLY

Annoying pest buzzing by

Who knows where your feet have been?

Vomiting on people's dinner

Giving Wes hassle

He cannot concentrate

Swats you away

But you persist

You Annoying insect

I will get murderous at your presence

But you land as though mocking me

I go to kill you

You tease by hoping away and attacking my other arm

You put out your metaphorical tongue

And dare me to get you

Do not worry Mr Bluebottle

I'm going to address this misdemeanour

With some good old fashioned spray

And if that does not work

I will bash you with the can

And all your mates

So, you can be the filling

Of a Garibaldi biscuit

STRIFE

Let me make more of my life

I do not need you to fuel my strife

It is time to commit to a better quality of life

With or without my imagined wife

Love I find is such a weirdness

I have no clue what is going on I confess

Life should be a game of chess

Except its less organised- what a mess

Death for me will not be a happy release

Calling out to my spirit to leave me please

Brain melting like a pizza full of cheese

The outcome of this violent disease

Thinking logically caused me such pain

I cannot go through this again

Jumping through hoops to complete the chain

I have no energy to explain this refrain

WEDNESDAY

So, we have arrived at Wednesday

We are halfway there

Keeping an eye out for what will happen

Poor old Odin/Woden had to lose his eye for wisdom

A sacrifice of the mundane to gain the divine

Just how I feel about Wednesday

Halfway there- is it day 3 or 4

Moving on

We can be imaginative like in Germany as it is 'middle of the week'-
Mittwoch

Or as fleet as Mercury and get the message across and wish ourselves a
happy mercredi

With the elegance of the gods' and be delivered on this day of Hermes

When it is all Greek to me!!!

PETROL PIRACY

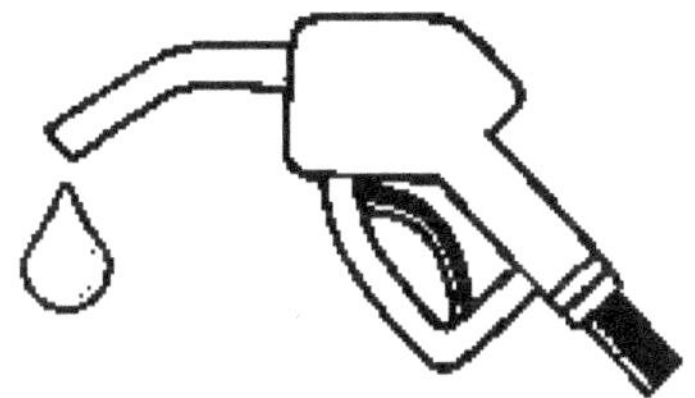

As they advance across the waves of traffic

Joining the queues of other privateers who are on a mission

We must fill the hold before everyone does

We are modern day prospectors

And this is a gold rush

The vehicles make their way

The people carriers

The Chelsea Tractors

The old chugalong that has not been exposed for ages

All in the relentless pursuit of fuel

Everyone is told it is not in short supply.

Just behave normally

But that does not apply to me

As I must have a full tank

And so must my daughter

And her boyfriend

And it becomes a daily ritual

Of pyjamaed slippered mothers

Dragging their child to a vendor of their chosen freedom

Because they say I can so I must

And Facebook has posted the latest delivery

Of the fruit of crude

Which makes everyone so so rude

Except the flags are waving saying none of the black gold here

Have we been Jolly Rogered?

Go on your journey of discovery elsewhere

Pieces of eight and octane fuelled rage

The tankers flow halted

Man overboard as the fighting from each vessel as they pass by

Perceived and real pushing in

And jumping the queue

As all reason is lost

As it was my turn

And I am more important than you with your blue light

And do you really want a fight

And do not tell me what to do

And the empty forecourts as all the treasure is gone

And then the real pirates emerge

This is my opportunity to make a buck

No longer 1.31 a litre but 1.42

To make up for the hassle

Of tending to your needs

And being closed during the pandemic

Except you stayed open

But people forget that

In your parroted voices

That spout sorrows

But feed on your greed

Because selfish people could not wait

And the sheep baa baa baa bleated

Causing a further cascade and up and down we go again

HALLOWEEN 2021

We are alarmed to find in this horror genre

That the child is reciting the old rhymes

Out of a leather bound book

That has been leafed through by the generations

And is sharing the words passed on through the mists of time

About malevolent spirits imbibing

And eating malleable products

Whilst being impaled on staves

And being smeared in the grease of non-vegan substances

Which does not stop dripping and dripping

With a ferocity unbounded

But this is no Halloween movie

Where incantations of past charms and spells bring forth the hell bound masses

But imaginations are wrecked by the hushed tones of parental rotes

The clanging like chains of the rhymes

Getting repeatedly louder and louder

Beating down on the eardrums of the listener

In monotonous tones and then whispering words

That may insert fear into the young

As the three little ghosties,

Which are sitting on posties,

Peruse the scenes before them

As the adult continues with the rhyme

Eating buttered toasties of unknown quantities

Greasing up their fisties which are fibrillating in anticipation

The hell fires from the shared imagination have charred the bread

But the devils have shaken the bovine meaty body to produce the spread and dripping

To give the meal a flavour for the phantoms to enjoy

Up to their wristies.

Oh, what beasties

To have such feasties

There is no more to be said except

Horror is so spooky

No god-fearing human would dare to ingest such a meal

As there is no marmite in sight

WHY DO WE WRITE?

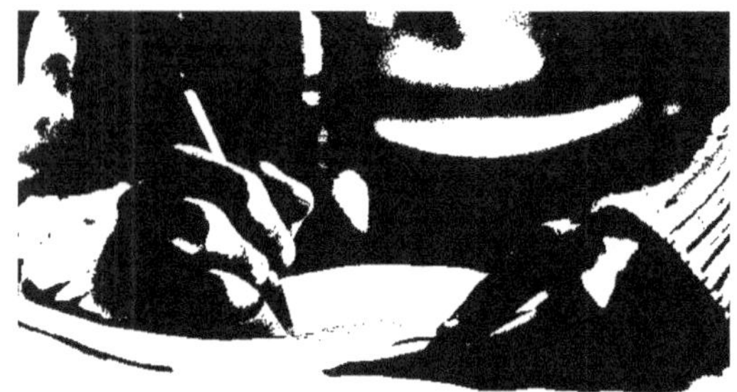

Why do we write?

Is it right?

Do we have the right?

To write about our rite

Our rite of passage

Our sacred rite

Which may be expressed as a prayerful right or rite

That is orated or written as the right thing to do

And it is therapeutic to write down our innermost thoughts

And have the right to do so

Built up on a history of fighting for our rights

Whether we be an old fashioned wordsmith or 'wright' or a new writer

And we reflect on our rite of writing

An underused craft that we muse on as we continue to write to manufacture our art form

As we look to the physical left and right for our inspiration

And comment on the political circumstances as we do not want to be right when all have is left

Being dextrous not sinister- see I used Latin roots as it is my right

We write as we have the right to share our rite of being a wright

To open our hearts to right the wrong

Because there is so much wrong to right

But the power of our pen is mighty as we write

It rips through evil like a righteous sword whether you be left or right handed

As we chose to conform or rebel against the perceived communal rite

As we come of age and express our personal rites

And mature into a writer about a righter of rights and rites

And that is why we write

Because it is our right to write about our rite being a wright

Ok-All right/write

HAPPY DAYS

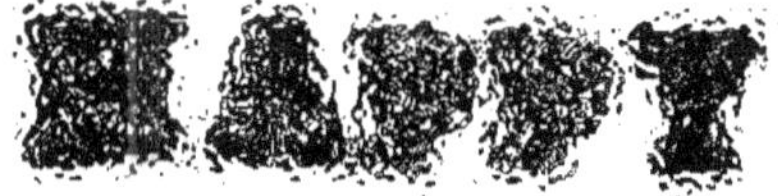

Today is a day to be happy

Why not celebrate this

We are not going to be negative because negativity breeds itself

Like a small amoeba splitting into two ad infinitum

Until it fills all our space and invades the love in others

Peoples beauty can be plucked from the eye of all the beholders present

And shared with everyone around to light their personal flames

We will work hard on ourselves to be this shining beacon a perpetual light

We will explore love and graft its cuttings like the philosophical gardeners that we are

So, it will continue to bloom and create new fruit for all to take in

We will write joyous words that sing alleluias and praise to our spirits

That we have created or have immersed ourselves in

We will not dwell on what has gone wrong but focus on what went right

We are our own army with our swords and shields of metaphorical weaponry

We are tacticians in this fight to live life -a dolce vita

Fear has no place as it is for weaklings, and we are strong

The internal burning of our different beliefs in ourselves provide fuel

The new creed will be reborn like a phoenix from its own ashes as nothing is destroyed but changed

We will be perfection in our own vision which is not blurred by negativity

Happiness is our mantra which we chant through our actions

Like a holiness in our personal faith

Our being is radiating the positivity as we meet with others

Collecting the gifts that we are given covertly and overtly

Today is a good day

And tomorrow will be too

I am sure

I am reborn

I am an optimist and I only see good ahead for us all

So, to repeat

Today is the day we are going to be happy

XMAS 2021

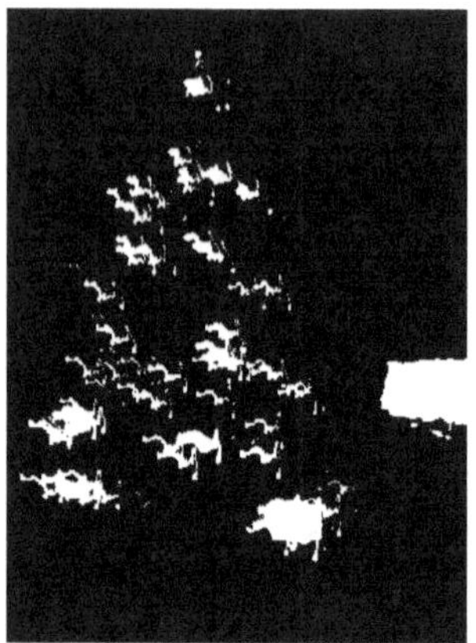

Merry Christmas is the words we all sing

Sharing our happiness is what we can bring

Love to all the world at this time of year

Food and wishing each other good cheer

Songs of joy and moods reflecting

Angelic voices always harmoniously chanting

The words of our thoughts and wishing you well

Hymns and carols accompanying the chiming bells

Gifts are wrapped and under the decorated tree

Excited children identity which ones for you and for me

Pressing, guessing from what shape they are

Seeing if they have been delivered from near or from far

Parents sharing their childhood memories of times of old

Magi reverently bringing the gifts of gold

Love is in the waft of myrrh and frankincense

Bright baby eyes show worlds view of innocence

Who says Christmas is just for the young?

The eternal mystery lost in our worldly pang

Adestes Fidelis the Latin hymn

Drawing the faithful into the light when the weather is grim

The Midnight Mass of new birth and hope

Celebrated universally in many tongues across the globe

And the remembrance for their spiritual sacrifice

Is to make sure that there are rewards for not being naughty but nice

THE SCARF

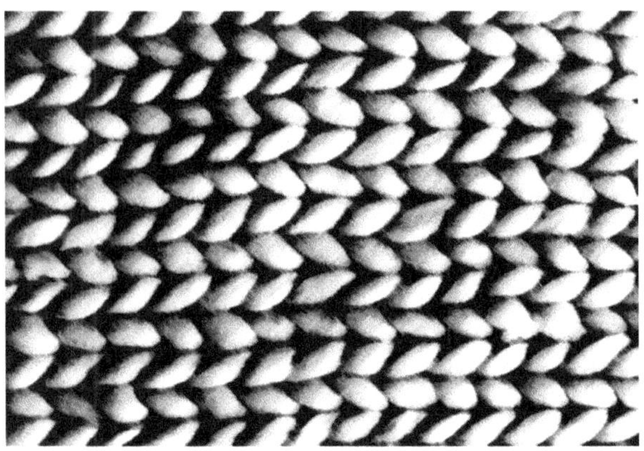

If I had a scarf of my own

I would wrap it around my own neck

It would provide me with the warmth I need on this freezing day

It would signify that I am looking after myself

And people would admire it from afar

Knowing that I follow the best sports team

Or that I have a penchant for a bright colour

And that it matches what I am wearing

Or totally clashes

Because that is what I want to show

That I am me and set my own fashion

And I no longer have to be vague about my life

Instead, I have no scarf

I am nothing

I have no identity

I am not wrapped snuggly by anything or anyone

Every day is cold

Even when the sun is out to supply warmth to me

I do not belong

So, if you see me

And you have a scarf to spare

Then lend it to me

Instead of wrapping it on a snowman or woman

You may even see my frail humanity

My bio-socio-psycho-emotional holistic being

I may even melt

Because I will see love in its true form

And not be another statistic going berserk on the streets

Causing havoc in your uncharitable world

Unlike the fallen snow

Which will melt away with no consequence

Like the rest of the inconsequential

Dripping down the drain with no understanding

I do not really need a physical woolly scarf

Just that I feel warm and cherished

The act of giving it is enough

And I may be able to reciprocate

And you will then receive a scarf from me

WHAT IS NOT PERSONAL?

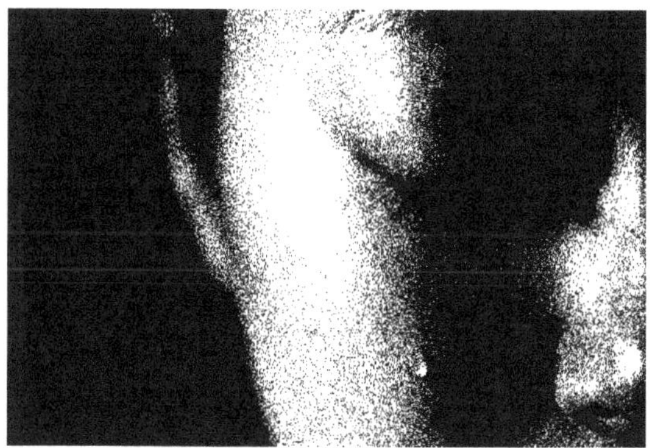

Well, we all have a go at the personnel

Who inhabit our lives

As they get personal

About what we do and who we are

They espouse their own humanity

And say that we are like an organisation's Human Resources

Except they are devoid of any humanity or resources

Their well is empty

Of empathy and support

And their skill levels are zero

They are no heroes

They say the family and friends' law is the law

The rules we go by

We are here to protect you

My friend my family

But it is usually one

The one who skives off

A worthless in my eyes

Speaking their lies into other ears

Loading the emotional gun

And bang -bang someone else fires it.

They deny being there in the first place

What me gov?

Never saw a thing!

And if I was there, it was coincidence

I was not the person who you saw doing anything wrong.

Inside I am my own person

I have multiple shields around myself which I allow others to penetrate
with permission

A number of the shields are of ice

Some are melting snow

Some are the flowing joy of a replenishing fluid.

When a personal attack is made

I freeze

I do not understand in that moment what to do

Do I defend myself

I relax

The waterfall reappears

It may be slightly tainted by the input you have made

Like an accidental drip of ink into a lake

But sometimes the fluid is frozen

And the hammering attacks give fractures to my protective field

The soothing flow is absent, and the rawness becomes clear to all

I feel alone in a room of many

Defenceless against the normality

Just because you say it is not personal

Does not mean that it is not hurting my damaged being more

Not making any repairs to my consciousness

Unconsciously I cannot cope

I make crying sounds

Beseeching you to help me

And aid with your personal strength against the perceived foes

But your distain shows me that it is indeed personal

HOPE 22

So, 2022 has arrived

With a whimper not a bang

Well, the doors were opened and closed, and good riddance paid to the year

All sorts of hope made in our resolutions unfulfilled

That we make again every year

No smoking or drinking

Cutting down on the meat pies

Or becoming a plant eater

Instead of just celebrating Life

Breathing in because we can

Chatting to a friend

Enjoying a drink and food because it is allowed

Focusing less on the errant politicians who know everything and does nothing

Will all acquaintance be forgot?

For auld lang syne

We go on

Because we want to

We have made our choices and celebrate that we are able to.

We can spend our day realistically confronting our fears

And supporting each other without prejudice of each other

Like we used to before the dreaded virus

We can be cathartic and allow ourselves to express our emotions of sadness and gladness in the safety of each other our friends and neighbours

In looking forward we can prescribe an enjoyable time for ourselves and others, whether that be in another place or be at home

As we are surviving, we can Inform others of our experience that the sun will rise tomorrow and that there will be a moon in the sky

We can reflect on what had happened and look to the future to allow ourselves to create what we want and be one of lives catalysts

GUTTER SNIPERS AIM AT WHAT?

Take aim and fire goes through my head

I cannot stop

The heat of anger burns me

I see my filthy jealousy pour along the pipes of my mind

Onto the broken carapace left before me

As you try to leave I aim at the target that is you

I use the only weapon I possess

My words

I am sarcastic

I am hateful

I know the button to press

I can make you react

And I see your hope running away

Not trickling but gushing

A torrent to match my speech

That is my power

I use it for evil

You want to move but you are petrified

You are a Stone

A monument to my vile actions

More filth gushes towards you

Like a putrid diarrhoea of verbs and nouns

I chose my projectile carefully

I am an oral sniper

My dictionary crafted in the gutter

The vocabulary honed to destroy

Bang goes my verbal bullet

One word

Hatred

It explodes

What heartstrings were left hanging, ping away

Your heart falls into the void- the chasm of darkness

I have hit the target

I am a sharpshooter

The gutter sniper of repute

BRIDAL PARTY

She thought that she heard "here comes the bride" as she walked up the aisle

It was the joy of the occasion creating a musical illusion as her father held her arm in arm as she took her steps towards her love

As each footstep was taken her heart swelled with pride

She could see her life partner standing at the end of the passage she was travelling

She knew that once she arrived that there would be no turning back

It was not because she was forced to be there against her will

It was her whole being willing her to complete the whole when two becomes one

It was not the Spice Girls playing in her ears but incidental music

Notes that they had chosen to announce her arrival at the point of matrimony

These notes became an anthem

A joy before family and friends

As they reached each other, the father's role was almost completed

He handed over his first born daughter to her future husband

He still had a vestige of control

He did not need to say the words to confirm he was giving her away.

But this was not the way their relationship had worked over the years

It had developed into an adult-to-adult interaction

He trusted her choices

He believed in her

He approved her choice

He saw the equality in life and remembered that he had borrowed her life from her birth until now

Now was the right time for a change.

The words "I will" easily formed on his lips

They flowed from his mouth as easily as the joyful tears fell from his eyes

They were temporarily parted as the rest of the words were shared between the lovers before him

All too soon the ceremony was over, and the new story of their lives began

SPACE

Space the imagined grace

You go to your happy place

You are alone

You are away from yourself

Circling the clouds

The amorphous gaining shape in your cognitive processes as you make sense of your surroundings

It had no bearing on your journey through life's wanderings

Except that you were fooling yourself again

You needed to gain a structure

To give yourself a running chance

You claim to be a rebel

You have no cause

You persist in this fantasy that you are hip to be cool

But your rebellion is old hat

You are hip to be square

Others have been there before you were born

Your reason to be, you feel no longer exists, so you are now destructive

Only to yourself

Your soul

Your being.

Your essence

Your physical self

You need to receive your self-love

Something that you manufactured on your own

Not rely on others to name you -to give you being

You are an individual with your own name

You can carve your own way in the world with your own space

Space is not your final frontier but a beginning.

TASTE THE EMOTION

I tasted love

It was fruity, spicy, rich like a dark sweet cake.

There were sounds interspersed like a wedding march in the past.

My joy fizzed as purple space dust popped onto my tongue, and I said those wonderous words

The cherry from 1980 reminded me that I had been young and remembered happiness

Instead, I now experienced hate

It was a hot spicy chilli as I expressed my anger to you

It burned so hot as I burned you

You looked at me with the Vicks vapour rub eyes

The sting as the raw emotion is bare before you

It hangs in the air unwanted but somehow useful to clear the air with its anaesthetic essence.

The Lone banana aroma sickly as you whispered a fake, I love you back

If there had been a mixture with toffee, then I would know that you meant it

Instead, it made me nauseous as I understood your emotions were not real

Sadness engulfed me with the saltiness of rotten peanuts or tinned anchovies

I then realised that I was allergic to you

My eyes red dripping and swelling with onion oozing from them

You didn't want me to see you go and find another who was your taste

Was I too old like lavender?

Or lost my fruitiness like a shrivelled orange

You made me spit out the flavour of you

The umami of marmite as I was unsure whether I loved or hated you

The sweetness tainted

The cake is crushed

It has no flavour

It was void

THE STAG

The day had finally arrived

The research crew assembled for the event

Making their way to the various airports across the UK for their gentle invasion of the Emerald Isle

But first sustenance to get the day started.

A belly full of your best fried products to line your stomach and prepare for the day ahead

Early research of the black fluid was made by the Caledonian contingent to set a baseline

After an uneventful flight and a bumpy landing

Further samples were obtained early on and assessed to check quality.

Field research was planned for the rest of the days to check the local distribution of the products for assessment of various variables including temperature colour consistency and of course volume.

The testers had been chosen for their ability to discern these properties consistently and with vigour.

All samples were evaluated, and initial results suggested that "there wasn't a bad pint amongst them"

Samples of other products were taken from the location which were independently evaluated by their named experts.

This may have caused a confusion in the results, but this was mitigated by taking account of the bias of the tester who expressed the view "I really don't drink beer"

There was a break in the tests to find another location where a different product was to be evaluated and testing needed to be recalibrated

This product had been used with the main product over the years and often referred to as a snifter or chaser

Again, all was confirmed, and some taken away for testing on another day

The evaluation visits were concluded, and testers were free to taste as many samples to their hearts content and sort out the world.

SHANTY

Cutting my craft through the spray -so grey

Sailing my boat red and blue

Getting lost in the foam so monochrome

To find my way back home to you

Yo Ho bottles of beer

Sitting my ass on the planks

Making my way through the white spray

For the eternal embraces with you

 My brain is fuddled -so very muddled

Full of the briny Med salt

Waiting expectations -in this united nation

My heartbeat does somersaults

Sailing through waters -getting gifts for your daughters

Avoiding the scary monsters there

Amongst multiple chatting -chanting prayers in Latin

Avoiding the Mal de Mer there

Happy to arrive in one piece- I'm alive

Seeing my own native land

I express my joy –as a man not a boy

As you take me in your loving hands

AMERICANISMS

Your words have invaded the language from Dr Kildare and Starsky and Hutch

Sesame Street has changed our tone and imbued us with the Spanish Language.

We have to have the cajones to make a decision instead of the balls

In everyday speech I can't find u

There is something missing from color

You have no honor

Your candor at sharing what is happening is partially missing

Even your armor against life is missing a vital part.

You have adapted your words by making simplistic describers such as sidewalks

Or overcomplicated our spoken word by having multiples such as escalator or elevator while moving stairs or lift will do.

You love to change the technical by substituting a K for a C

Just because Sauerkraut has a K doesn't mean that cabbage has to

Or my beating heart going back to its Greek from Latin roots when we get an EKG or epinephrine instead of adrenaline

We seem to have ended up in the ER instead of Casualty or A+E

We have lost the theatrical experience of the OR

I go through the alphabet from A to Zed or is it Zee

Or use a Z for a S so I can emphasise or is it emphasize or am I getting so confused

Who do the forces report to as they defend me?

Does it have a C or is it an S?

I'd get into trouble if I tried to erase my pencil marks with a condom when I asked for a rubber

Is it garbage or just rubbish?

I just wanted some chips, but they seem to be sold in a convenience store that is not always very convenient.

What I really wanted is called French fries which have never been near the continent.

Farah Hot Tap Majors not Faucet

The film moves, the season falls

My vegetables are no longer French but Italian as I make my ratatouille with a plant of eggs

Or beets instead of beetroot

At least Trump is the same in both languages to describe a fart or emission of hot air

And I can rest in the toilet

Two countries separated by a language.

Thanks George Bernard Shaw -An Irishman who understood English

PARTIES

Boris Johnson is a fat buffoon

We know that coming soon

The publishing world will burst the inflated balloon

Because the time of reckoning is nigh, high noon

No use wrapping yourself in a cocoon

Ignoring what will be your doom

As all the parties were caught on Zoom

And more than socially distanced was in the room

Or in the back garden boom-boom

Like cheating in the common room

Your reputation like litter strewn

You pretend to all about being immune

We thought it was going to be a honeymoon

Promised if we obeyed it would be over in June

Instead, you played cards with our life like poker or pontoon

Or if you want to be up market Vingt et un

As you spun the roulette wheel and gambled with our sanity every afternoon

With the speeches from scientists to allay our doom

But you fed us crap from a spoon

Be gone so we can listen to a new tune.

THE CANDLE

I am lit by your light

I know that this is right

You are odourless

You tell me what I need to know

It comes from your glow

You have a little heat

But I dare not touch you again

As I will feel pain

I will reflect on this as I feel real

Happy, sad, I can share what I am

I can see my fortune in your flame flicker

I could think much quicker

If my life were better, I could be slicker

I hear your voice

As I made my choice

Did I have a chance?

As you led me a merry dance

Puff you are out!!!

Dead but a lingering smoke trail where you were

HAPPINESS

Today is the day to write

I am clearing out my head

Making a space for me

I am finding out about myself

It is time to be 'nosey' about me

I am usually looking at others as I am interested

Or is this just stalking

Anyway, I know that I put people in boxes

Boxes that I have made myself psychologically

And added labels to them so I can find them again

And then make further judgements

I need to be more open

Which is why I am clearing out my head

The detritus that I have collected

I need the space to walk around inside myself

Have a wander around and find things

Stuff that I may have lost or don't know that I have lost yet

Meandering in the breeze will be fun

Exciting, scary but fun

I have to let go- not hold on

It has to be a good clear out

I find that I am correcting myself when I need to take a risk

I bless myself that I allow myself to do this

I need to adopt a new style

Take the bull by the horns

I find myself judging me

In the absence of judging others

I worry that I will offend you by speaking my truth

But my lack of vocalising what I want to say just gets put into another box and added to the baggage.

Think now speak later maybe fine at times

Today I take the time- take the risk

Purge myself of the sadness

Share what needs to be shared with others

Not all the gifts will be wanted, but it is better to give than receive

This is my moment, my cathartic moment

I have a chance to say what I want to

My reality

My happiness

I will be funny now

Not later

INDEX

ABOUT THE AUTHOR

Joseph Campling moved from the New Town of Bracknell to the town of Slough to train as a nurse in the mid 1980's. During that period, he had to mature from one of life's innocents into the man he is now (whatever that is!!)

Having worked initially within an operating theatre as a scrub nurse, he then re-qualified as a mental health nurse and has worked in various roles ranging from older people with dementia to younger people with serious mental health issues. Whilst undertaking his BSc, he was one of three co-authors of an article which was published in a professional journal in 2007.

As a child he was a voracious reader, and it is reported (by his mother) that he could read at the age of two and loved English Language and Literature. He first drafted a poem about a scarecrow at the age of 9 and followed it up with a poem (name unknown) which had a line about a woman being swallowed by a crocodile while still having her handbag on her arm. However, when O' levels came around he was put into the CSE class where he ended up with a level 2. Knocking the 'chip off his shoulder' he gained an English qualification which enabled him to move on in life. He also authored poems which do not survive.

From 2010 he found himself scribbling his thoughts down on bits of paper, envelopes, and his mobile phone which thanks to 'modern technology' he was able to keep safe. At the age of 50, he also discovered open mic, but due to having the singing voice of a frog being strangled and the guitar skills to match, he resorted to reading out some of this saved work.

Early on in his performing life, he experienced being heckled. However, the heckler's wife asked that he read out a Pam Ayres poem (I Wished I'd Looked After My Teeth). To please her he did so. The following week, the heckler's wife heckled someone else with "Get the poet on" so he knew he had 'made it'!!

Having extended his performing venues thanks to Spoken Word events, he has seen multiple forms of poetry and verse and has evolved from rhyming everything to being much freer in his expression. He is often found 'scribbling' and then performing what he has just written. Last year he collaborated with a jazz composer by writing lyrics which he put to music. Hopefully, there will be further work completed soon.

In May 2018 he self- published "Mild Musings May Mitigate My Mentality" which was his first collection of poems and having learned from the process has published another volume of 'words' "Merring or is it Mrs Gren." The title came from a conversation which the author had with his daughter about a mnemonic to remember the seven signs of life.

Outside writing and performing, his interests include history, watching live music, trying to play the guitar (still project in progress) and quizzing. He also likes to watch TV; mostly factual documentaries, comedy and quiz shows. He also 'hangs out' with members of the local drama club which is his family's passion, although he has no plans to act. He also needs to read more and swears that he will do so very soon as he has a pile of books to read. He follows rugby and can sometimes be found cheering his team on (London Irish) whether they win or lose. He also has a passion for Liverpool Football Club.

Jofuss
Camelyne
Publishing

www.ingramcontent.com/pod-product-compliance
Lightning Source LLC
Chambersburg PA
CBHW072055150726
47999CB00005B/1790